The Learning Works

Create a National Park

A Complete Unit for Students to Use in Creating an Original National Park

Grades 4–8

Written by Charlotte Jaffe and Barbara Doherty
Illustrated by Beverly Armstrong

The Learning Works

Cover Design & Illustration:
Bev Armstrong

Editing and Text Design:
Clark Editorial & Design

Copyright © 1998
The Learning Works, Inc.
Santa Barbara, California 93160

ISBN: 0-88160-292-2
LW 362

Printed in the United States of America.

Table of Contents

SECTION I • Our National Parks

Acadia National Park

Everglades National Park

Mesa Verde National Park

Yellowstone National Park

Table of Contents
(continued)

Table of Contents
(continued)

Teacher Overview

Create a National Park is an exciting and challenging unit that provides background information about the United States National Park System. The information and activities in this book also encourage students to develop an understanding that these unique park areas must be permanently protected and maintained. After learning about our existing parks, the class divides into cooperative learning groups of three to five students in order to create their own national parks. Work on this project can be done during class periods and as homework assignments. A culminating activity, "National Park Day," is an opportunity for student groups to share the information they have learned and the projects they have created. During "National Park Day," student groups can also perform skits they have written for classmates, family members, teachers, and administrators.

As a result of participating in this unit of study, students will gain practice in the following skills:

- analyzing
- comparing and contrasting
- decision-making
- evaluating
- hypothesizing
- planning and organizing

- problem solving
- creative thinking
- critical thinking
- script-writing techniques
- dramatics
- public speaking

Text Overview

Create a National Park is divided into five sections.

Section I • Our National Parks

Five national parks and one national historical park are profiled in this section: Acadia National Park, Everglades National Park, Mesa Verde National Park, Yellowstone National Park, Yosemite National Park, and Independence National Historical Park. Topic headings in this section are History, Wildlife, Plant Life, Location and Physical Features, Conservation Concerns, and Special Features and Exhibits. Student activities listed on each page provide the opportunity for critical and creative thinking about the information provided. You may choose one or all of the activities for the students to complete. A "national parks sharing period" should be held once a week so that students can discuss their completed activity work with their classmates.

Teacher Overview
(continued)

Section II • Create Your Own National Park

The activities in this section help students to formulate their ideas about an imaginary national park. These cooperative activities include writing activities and project starters. Students are challenged to design a map of their national park and to create travel posters. Information brochures that discuss special features and activities and describe park facilities are also created by student groups. Students are required to design handouts that describe environmental or conservation concerns pertaining to their parks. These activities also involve students in brainstorming ideas for models, games, dioramas, and other projects. Each group will also compose an encyclopedia entry for their national park.

Section III • Create a Skit

In this section, each cooperative learning group has the responsibility of writing a skit that is set in its national park. After considering plot, characters, dialogue, and format, each group will choose one member to be a scribe and write the skit using the ideas of the whole group. Each group can create props and costumes to enhance their skit. A rehearsal schedule can be made by the group. The skits are to be performed on "National Park Day."

Section IV • National Park Day

The pages in this section contain directions for preparing and setting up displays for "National Park Day." Activities include creating invitations, completing planning sheets and sketches, and writing thank-you letters.

Section V • Park Potpourri

This section contains general information about national parks, a biographical sketch of John Muir, maps, descriptions for several national park careers, selected park addresses, and a list of reference materials.

Student Overview

The National Park System includes 369 sites found throughout the United States in forests, deserts, prairies, mountains, wetlands, and even cities. Some parks feature breathtaking scenery or unusual plants and wildlife, while others honor people and places of American history. Some of the parks are enormous, covering thousands of acres, while others are quite small.

Imagine that you and a group of fellow students have been asked to create a new national park in the location of your choice. You will be able to map your park, and describe its history, environment, weather conditions, and conservation concerns. You will design posters, brochures, and signs for your park as well as completing other fun activities such as inventing a game to teach others about your park.

Along with creating your own national park, this book provides an opportunity for you to work with a group of students to develop a skit that takes place in your park. As a concluding activity, your group will present your skit and other information about your park during a special presentation called "National Park Day."

As you gather information about our unique national park system and develop your own creative national park ideas, you will begin to understand the importance of protecting and preserving these special places for future generations.

Section I
Our National Parks

Acadia National Park

History

Before the arrival of Europeans, most of the state of Maine was inhabited by thousands of Native Americans. They were mostly of the Algonquian language group: Penobscots, Passamoquoddies, Abnaki, and Etchemin. Evidence of their encampments shows that they were living here approximately 6,000 years ago.

In 1604, the French explorer, Samuel de Champlain sailed past the shores of this area. For a long while, control of the area was passed back and forth between the French and the English. Jesuit priests established a mission in 1613, but it only survived about a year. There was a settlement of English here prior to the formation of the pilgrim colony of Massachusetts. After the end of the French and Indian Wars, settlers moved from the southern New England colonies to live in Maine. In 1820, when Maine became a state, the area now called Mount Desert Island was still mostly unknown. By 1900 it had become a fashionable summer resort. Many wealthy people built their summer "cottages" here. In 1903, one of these summer residents donated a small piece of his property for public use. Other wealthy landowners followed his example. By 1919, the area was formed into a national park. This was the first park donated to the United States government.

Activities

1. Learn about the people who donated the land for Acadia National Park. Find out what their "cottages" were like.

2. Imagine that you are on board Champlain's ship sailing along the rocky Atlantic coast. Write an entry for the ship's log.

3. Read *The Sign of the Beaver* by Elizabeth George Speare. This book tells the story of a family moving from Massachusetts to Maine in the 1700s.

Acadia National Park

Location

Acadia National Park is situated approximately three miles from Bar Harbor, Maine, on the rocky Atlantic coast. It is within 50 miles of Bangor, Maine, and within a day's drive of other major population centers of the east coast. The visitors' center is located at Hulls Cove on Maine Route 3. Part of this park is on the mainland and the rest of the park is made up of islands, beaches, waterways, and the Schoodic Peninsula.

Physical Features

Vistas here of rugged coastlines are truly breathtaking. In some places, the Atlantic Ocean comes crashing against the cliffsides; at other places, the surf meets the beach more gently. More than 120 miles of trails take the walker or hiker through forests, over mountains, and along rocky beaches, marshes, and bogs. A lake formed by glacier action makes a wonderful spot for fishing. The paths around Eagle Lake are ideal for horseback riding, carriage rides, or walking. Cadillac Mountain, with its pink granite summit is 1,530 feet above sea level. This is the highest point directly on the Atlantic coast. You will also find Somes Sound, the only true fjord in America outside of Alaska. This body of water cuts into Mount Desert, creating the look of a lobster claw. Another popular spot with visitors is Thunder Hole. This narrow opening in the rocky coast makes a sound like thunder when the wind, waves, and tide combine in just the right way to squeeze air until it "explodes." Acadia National Park is made up of more than 40 square miles of varied natural beauty.

Activities

1. Create a travel poster or advertisement for Acadia National Park.

2. Do research to learn more about the pathway system around Eagle Lake.

3. Define the word *fjord*. Draw a picture of a fjord.

Create a National Park
© The Learning Works, Inc.

Acadia National Park

Wildlife

The varied habitats of Acadia National Park support a great range of wild-life—from salamanders to humpback whales. There are 45 species of land mammals, 12 species of marine mammals, 338 kinds of birds, 17 species of amphibians, and a great number of freshwater fishes. Visitors can find gray tree frogs, snapping turtles, shrews, moles, bats, black bears, raccoons, minks, skunks, coyotes, red foxes, Eastern timber wolves, and bobcats, among other species. The woods, lakes, and meadows of Acadia are also home to white-tailed deer, moose, Eastern woodland caribou, and American elk.

The sea is home to harbor and gray seals; harbor porpoises; two types of dolphins; whales, including pilot, finback, minke, humpback, right, and beluga, as well as the orca. In addition, visitors and residents enjoy the lobster, scallops, crabs, and clams caught locally. In the tidal pools and along the edge of the ocean, green sea urchins, Northern starfish, rock crabs, and mussels can be found. Eider ducks and herring gulls are common sights.

Activities

1. Compare two of the species of whales found in the waters of Acadia National Park.

2. Make a poster showing a food chain among some of the species found at Acadia.

3. Of the animals listed above, make a list of the 10 you find most interesting. Explain your choices.

Acadia National Park

Plant Life

Acadia is home to a wide variety of plant life. Blueberry bushes can be found throughout the park. There are many types of flowering plants to be found, including lupines, trillium, lady's-slipper, trailing arbutus, bunch-berry (a type of dogwood), jewelweed, harebell, wild rose, cranberries, rasp-berries, iris, water lilies, and honeysuckle. Kelp, mosses, and other water plants are found in and near the ocean. Forest and ocean come together dramatically along Acadia's coastline.

Evergreen trees were the predominant type of tree in Acadia until a great fire occurred in 1947. When the evergreens burned, the shade they pro-vided disappeared as well. Sun-loving species of trees grew in their place. These trees include the pin cherry, quaking aspen, silver birch, gray birch, maples, and tamarack.

There are several varieties of spruce, including the towering 60-foot red spruce. The pines are well represented with the white, pitch, jack, and red pine. Some of these trees appear in stunted form and in grotesque shapes. This is caused by the salt air, by the constant battering of the winds, and by growing conditions that are less than ideal.

Activities

1. Using 3 x 5 cards, make a small sketchbook and illustrate five plant or tree species of Acadia.

2. The tamarack is an interesting tree. Do research to discover what makes it unusual.

3. How would you encourage visitors to enjoy *and* protect the park's plant life? Brainstorm a list of ideas.

Acadia National Park

Conservation Concerns

Acadia National Park is home to several endangered and threatened plant and animal species. (Endangered animals are those likely to become extinct. Threatened animals are those likely to become endangered.) These plants and animals are protected and monitored at Acadia. Among the endangered animals are bald eagles, peregrine falcons, and harlequin ducks. There are 38 plant and 59 animal species that are given special protection by the state of Maine. The wetlands areas of Acadia are part of the Atlantic flyway, an important area for nesting and migrating birds.

The quality of the air is an important concern here. Pollution contaminates the park air due to the park's proximity to major centers of population and emissions from vehicle traffic. Another threat to the natural plants is posed by exotic plants (those that are not native to the area). Some exotic plants have been introduced by airborne seeds from local residents' gardens. The wild growth of one, the purple loosetrife, is crowding the growth of the native plants.

The preservation of the water quality is also very important. The Bass Harbor Marsh was polluted by a landfill that was located outside the park. The water quality is tested often, as some of the larger lakes are the source of public water supplies for nearby towns.

Historic buildings in the park are also a conservation concern. There are thousands of artifacts in several collections throughout the park.

Of special concern for preserving and conserving the park is the fact that the year-round population in the surrounding towns is increasing. Additionally, the demand for homes for summer use has increased by 50 percent. This has placed great pressure on the park. As more and more land is developed, the "buffer zones" are becoming smaller and smaller. Finding ways for people to enjoy the park without harming it is always a problem.

Activities

1. Draw a picture of the purple loosestrife.

2. Write a law which will be fair, yet limits development near the park.

3. Do research to find out more about the harlequin duck and write a short report about it.

Acadia National Park

Special Features

Robert Abbe Museum: This museum is home to a collection and exhibits of Native American artifacts.

Islesford Historical Museum: Here visitors can learn the story of early local settlers. Exhibits show a life-style which changed very little in 150 years. Settlers harvested the forests and the sea. They built ships, cut lumber, and farmed the fertile soils.

Baker Island and Bear Island Lighthouses: These lighthouses have been listed on the National Register of Historic Places.

The Carriage Roads: About 100 years ago, broken stone roads were commonly built. Fifty-five miles of these rustic roads wind up around the mountains and down through the valleys. They were specially designed for horses or horse-drawn carriages, not motor vehicles.

Mount Desert Island: Two major valleys were created by glacier action on the island. This same action made lakes in the valleys. The Abnaki Indians fished and collected the abundant shellfish here. In the late 1800s many artists came here to be inspired by the island's dramatic and rugged beauty. They transferred this beauty to their canvases. The island's popularity spread and it became a favorite summer retreat.

Activities

1. Do research to learn about some of the artists who painted the scenery of Mount Desert Island. Try to find some examples of their work. Share your findings with your classmates.

2. Make a map of Mount Desert Island. Identify Cadillac Mountain, Somes Sound, and Thunder Hole.

3. Who was John D. Rockefeller, Jr.? Write a short summary of his role in forming Acadia National Park.

Create a National Park
© The Learning Works, Inc.

Everglades National Park

History

Long ago an Indian tribe called the Glades inhabited the Everglades area. The tribesmen were excellent shell and wood carvers, and they fashioned their tools and weapons from these materials. The land was taken over by Spanish explorers during the beginning of the sixteenth century. For several hundred years the Spanish ruled, and the Glades Indians could not recapture the land from the powerful invaders. After the American Revolution, an Indian tribe called the Miccosukee moved into the territory of the Everglades and Big Cypress. Their descendants still live in the same territory today. These Indians were part of the larger Seminole nation, and they enjoyed hunting and fishing in what is now Everglades National Park. After Florida became an American territory in 1821, Indians from the Creek Confederacy also moved to the area. They set up orange groves and raised cattle. The Everglades still remained a wilderness area after the Civil War, with only a few Indian camps dotting the region. On December 6, 1947, Everglades became an authorized national park. It was established to protect the largest subtropical wilderness area in America.

Activities

1. Use the facts of the establishment of Everglades National Park to create a legend about the Glades Indians.

2. Imagine that you are a member of one of the Indian tribes that inhabited the Everglades area. Describe your surroundings. How did you feel when the Spaniards arrived?

3. Make a timeline and record the ways that the Everglades area has changed through the years.

4. Do research to learn about Marjory Stoneman Douglas, author of *The Everglades: River of Grass*. Find out how she fought to preserve the Everglades.

Everglades National Park

Location

Everglades National Park is located at the southern tip of the Everglades in southern Florida, about 50 miles from Miami. The main entrance to the park is in Homestead, southwest of Florida City. Big Cypress National Preserve, Biscayne National Park, and Dry Tortugas National Park are smaller areas that are located close to Everglades. Dry Tortugas is only accessible by seaplane or by boat.

Physical Features

Everglades National Park is filled with wondrous waterways. The main waterway is more than 100 miles in length—a marshy river that flows from Lake Okeechobee to the Gulf of Mexico. The Seminoles named it "Grassy Waters."

Miles of winding mangrove swamps and sawgrass marshes occupy a major portion of the park area. On elevated islands called hammocks, hardwood trees grow large and the vegetation is lush. Everglades National Park is the largest subtropical wilderness in America, and is home to many unique plant and animal species.

Activities

1. Do research to learn how the acquisition of Big Cypress National Preserve has helped the water problem at the Everglades.

2. Make a salt-and-flour map of Everglades National Park.

3. Create a model of a hammock showing its vegetation. Write a short report about the hammock.

4. The Everglades "back country" area has many interesting sites including Alligator Creek, Plate Creek, and the Nightmare. Write a short story with a mystery theme using one of these sites in the title of your story.

Everglades National Park

Wildlife

Warmed by the subtropical climate of South Florida, Everglades National Park sustains many species of animal life. Alligators, popular park attractions, live and move freely in the natural environment of the park's setting. Visitors are reminded to keep a distance of 15 feet away when viewing alligators and never to feed them.

Everglades National Park is home to more than 300 species of birds. Many have tropical origins and are very rare. The wood storks, large white birds with black-tipped wings, are the only storks in America. In the marshy water they feed by touch, not by sight. This unusual bird was placed on the Endangered Species list in 1984. Other water birds in the park are the roseate spoonbill (another declining species), the great white heron, the great blue heron, the reddish egret, and the snowy egret. The white ibis is the most common of the water birds in the Everglades. Flamingos flock along the south coast of the park. Near the mangrove islands, ospreys, pelicans, and cormorants make their nests.

The Florida panther, the loggerhead turtle, and the crocodile are park residents that are on the endangered or threatened animals list. Their numbers have diminished because of hunting and because of the construction of nearby human habitats. Another protected species is the manatee. These large mammals are unable to move fast enough to avoid collisions with power boats.

Twenty-six species of snakes, some venomous like the rattlesnake, can be spotted around the park. Raccoons are abundant and often are attracted to food stored at campsites. More than 300 types of fishes are found in the waters of the Everglades. Exotic fishes called cichlids, originally found in Central America, are now spreading rapidly in the waters throughout the park. The Everglades is said to be "the first national park preserved primarily for its abundance and variety of life."

Activities

1. Discuss the importance of the fish population in the Everglades. How is it vital to the park's ecosystem?

2. Make a mobile of your favorite Everglades animal species.

3. Write a fictional story about a personal experience with wildlife in the Everglades.

Everglades National Park

Plant Life

Everglades National Park harbors a great variety of distinctive plant life because it is a subtropical wilderness. Many tropical plants and trees are found on small elevated islands called hammocks. The largest living mahogany tree in America is located on Mahogany Hammock. Other hardwood trees found on hammocks include the crabwood, fiddlewood, and leadwood. The fine woods from these trees are often used in cabinetry work. Tropical strap ferns and other fern species also grow on the hammocks. The beauty berry, a shrub with a bright pink berry, can be spotted on the dense tropical hammocks along with a copper-colored tree called the gumbo-limbo.

Native palm trees are commonly seen throughout the park. Some of the interesting varieties include the coconut palm, the cabbage palmetto, the silver palm, and the saw-cabbage palm. Many species of colorful orchids contribute to the beauty of the area. Bromeliads such as spanish moss and wild pineapples are common in parts of the park. Cacti and yucca plants, usually found in arid areas, are plentiful along coastal parts of the park and on the dry hammocks.

Three kinds of mangrove trees—red, white, and black—are found in the swampy sections of the park. The three types grow close together in some areas, and elsewhere grow separately. The red mangrove is more common along the southern edge of the Everglades. Hurricanes have caused problems for plant life in the park. Some of the tall hardwood trees were lost when Hurricane Andrew hit in 1992. Hurricane Donna destroyed the mistletoe cactus in 1960.

Activities

1. Categorize the variety of plant life found in the Everglades.

2. Make a chart of seasonal effects on plant life in the park.

3. Research the poisonous vegetation in the park. The poisonwood is one example. Create a poster warning visitors about poisonous park plants.

4. Plan a trip that you would like to take to the Everglades. Chart your course on a map. Make a sketchbook of plants, animals, and other interesting things you might see on your trip.

Everglades National Park

Conservation Concerns

One of the greatest dangers that Everglades National Park faces is the loss of water that has been diverted from it to supply more populated areas in Florida's cities. As urban growth has increased, the habitats that need water to survive are being drained. The construction of canals and dikes has disrupted the life cycles of many plants and animals and threatened their existence. Another danger is posed by pollution. Because of pesticides, herbicides, and other chemicals in nearby industrial and agricultural centers, many fish of the Everglades contain high levels of mercury. Threatened species in the area of Everglades National Park include the American alligator, the green sea turtle, and the crocodile. Populations of water birds such as the ibis and herons have been reduced and need protection. The Everglades is also home to many rare plant species which should be preserved.

Activities

1. After careful research, make a chart of the ecosystem of Everglades National Park. Show how plants and animals depend upon each other.

2. Choose one environmental problem affecting the park, and write a letter to the editor of *"The Everglades Examiner"* expressing your feelings about the problem.

3. Have a class debate about a conservation issue facing Everglades National Park.

4. Make a list of the ways individuals can take action to improve the situation at Everglades National Park.

Everglades National Park

Special Features

When tourists visit Everglades National Park, a favorite stop is Anhinga Trail. This elevated boardwalk trail offers an excellent view of the park's wildlife, including alligators and unusual tropical birds. The Gumbo Limbo Trail is another popular walkway that crosses a hardwood hammock. Along the Gulf Coast area of the park, boat tours take visitors through the mangrove estuary and Ten Thousand Islands.

In Shark Valley, the northwestern section of the park, slough slogging or water walking through the sawgrass prairie is a challenging experience. Wet to the waist, the water walker is able to view alligator holes and cypress domes in the sawgrass marshes. The Wilderness Waterway in the back country part of the park offers many opportunities for canoers and other boaters to enjoy the spectacular scenery and wildlife. Whether boating, walking, or on a tram tour, visitors are given a unique view of the plant and animal diversity in the fragile but astonishing subtropical eco-zone of Everglades National Park.

Activities

1. Pretend that you are a park naturalist and lead a nature walk along one of the park's popular trails. Write your agenda. Describe the sights and wildlife that your visitors will observe.

2. What is a *cypress dome*? Draw a picture of a cypress dome.

3. Create a brochure for Everglades National Park. Include information about tram tours, walking trails, biking trails, and boating trips.

Mesa Verde National Park

History

The region that is now known as Mesa Verde National Park in Colorado was first occupied by Nomadic hunters around the first century A.D. These early inhabitants were basket makers and they lived in valleys and caves. The Basketmaker Period lasted until about A.D. 500. The early people hunted deer and elk using a spear-like weapon called an *atlatl*.

The Modified Basketmaker Period followed, from A.D. 500–750. During this time, the Anasazi became farmers and grew beans and corn. They learned how to make pottery and cook their food in the pots. For hunting, the Anasazi used the bow and arrow. The Indians lived in pithouses that were built in caves and on top of mesas. These structures had low walls with flat roofs that were held up by mud-covered poles. The people used ladders to enter and exit through an opening in the roof of the house.

The Developmental Pueblo Period lasted for the next 350 years. The houses were made of sandstone and stood in a curved row around a courtyard. Sometimes these houses had 50 or more rooms. The people became more skillful masons and potters. Farming techniques also improved.

From approximately A.D. 1100–1300 was the Great or Classic Period in Mesa Verde's history. The stone walls of the large pueblos were constructed of fine materials. Kivas were built inside the houses at this time. The Anasazi designed black and white pottery, colorful jewelry, and woven material. In the middle of this period, the Anasazi began to build their homes in the caves in the canyon walls, probably for protection. The Cliff House was the largest construction, containing more than 200 rooms. Many cliff homes had designs painted on the walls. Mysteriously, the cliff homes were abandoned by A.D. 1300.

In 1874, the cliff house in Ute Mountain Tribal Park was entered by W. H. Jackson, a photographer for the U.S. Geological and Geographic Survey. Another major discovery came in 1888, when Richard Wetherill and Charles Mason came upon the Cliff House and other Anasazi dwellings. More ancient ruins were subsequently discovered in the area. After interested citizens lobbied Congress, President Theodore Roosevelt signed a bill making Mesa Verde a National Park in 1906.

Activities

1. With your classmates, think of some possible explanations as to why the Anasazi abandoned their homes.

2. Create a basket or a piece of pottery like those produced by the Anasazi.

Mesa Verde National Park

Location

Mesa Verde National Park is situated in southwestern Colorado. The main entrance to the park lies between the cities of Cortez and Mancos. The Far View Visitor Center is approximately 15 miles from the main entrance, and the Chapin Mesa is about 21 miles away.

Physical Features

- The park is filled with high mesas and rugged deep-walled canyons. Wetherill Mesa, Chapin Mesa, Morefield Canyon, Prater Canyon, and Moccasin Canyon are some of the notable ones.

- Spectacular sandstone cliffs with arched cave areas are the settings for the focal point of the park—the mysterious cliff dwellings.

- Mesa Verde National Park is bordered by the Ute Mountain Indian Reservation. An unusual feature is the Sleeping Ute Mountain, which has the image of a man lying on his back.

- Within the park is Park Point Lookout, which offers excellent views of four states: Arizona, Colorado, New Mexico, and Utah.

Activities

1. Prepare a "Children's Walk" for younger visitors to Mesa Verde. Draw a trail map and highlight the sites that you think younger children would find most interesting.

2. Make a collage of different painted or drawn scenes of Mesa Verde. Hang it on a classroom bulletin board.

3. Create a papier-mâché or clay model of one of the physical features listed above.

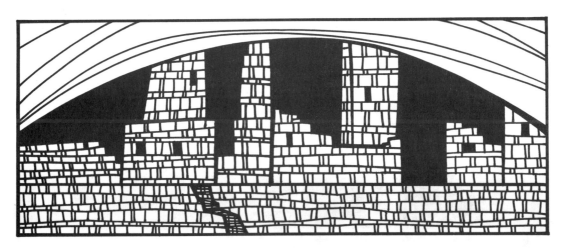

Create a National Park
© The Learning Works, Inc.

Mesa Verde National Park

Wildlife

A wide variety of wildlife inhabit the Mesa Verde area today. Some species, such as mule deer, turkey vultures, ravens, and jaybirds, may have also been residents long ago. Some animals have changed their habitats since the days of the Anasazi. When the Indians occupied the area, they cleared the land of underbrush and jackrabbits were abundant. Now that the brush once again covers the open land, cottontails are often seen on the mesa, while the jackrabbits still prefer the open valley fields. Mammals of all sizes—from bats and rodents to foxes, bighorn sheep, and mountain lions—share the park area with reptiles such as rattlesnakes and horned lizards. Migrant black bears have also been spotted as have herds of elk.

More than 180 species of birds live permanently in the park or migrate there during the spring, summer, or fall seasons. Commonly-seen species include the golden eagle, pinyon jay, great horned owl, and turkey vulture. Park visitors and rangers occasionally spot rare wood storks, snow geese, and painted buntings. The threatened southern bald eagle is found in the park, and endangered peregrine and prairie falcons soar through its wide-open skies.

The high mesa tops, deep canyons, and river areas offer a diverse habitat for the wildlife of Mesa Verde National Park.

Activities

1. Create a wildlife-spotter's checklist for park visitors. Include pictures of your favorite species. (These could be drawn, copied/cut from magazines, or done with stickers.)

2. Some petroglyphs contain carved pictures of animals that once lived in Mesa Verde. Create your own wildlife petroglyph picture and write a story to explain it.

3. Make a wildlife poster advertising Mesa Verde National Park.

Mesa Verde National Park

Plant Life

Mesa Verde Park got its name from the Utah Juniper and pinyon pine found in the canyons and on top of the mesa. Mesa Verde means "green table" in Spanish. The cones of the pinyon pine contain oily seeds and it is believed these seeds were consumed by the Anasazi. They used the pitch from the trees to waterproof their baskets. Another popular park tree is the Gambel oak, a tall tree usually found near water. The Anasazi used the wood of this oak to make tools. Rabbitbrush, a common park shrub, is covered with yellow flowers in the late summer. The Anasazi used the twigs from this shrub to make their baskets.

The Anasazi made use of much of the vegetation in the area. Wild tarragon, which the Indians might have used to season their food, is still seen growing in the canyon meadows. Wood from the rocky mountain juniper and the mountain mahogany was used by the Anasazi for creating tools and building parts. The Douglas fir is the most commonly found conifer in Mesa Verde. Its wood was used by the early Indians for many projects. Bright pink flowers called Hayden's gilia are seen growing out of the soft gray shales at the bottom of the mesa, and the orange-reddish Indian paintbrush can be discovered along the Knife Edge Road in the park.

In the more arid Hovenweep area, plants and shrubs flourish. The Squawbush; the cliffrose, with its sweet-smelling flowers; the prickly pear cactus, and the big sagebrush are some of the species found in this region of the park. Throughout Mesa Verde National Park, the visitor can see a variety of beautiful landscapes.

Activities

1. Write a park bulletin telling park visitors what they should and should not do in order to preserve the vegetation of the environment.

2. Find out how the Anasazi used the following: Mormon tea, Indian rice grass, Utah serviceberry, and fendler bush.

3. Create a diorama showing the plant life in Mesa Verde.

Mesa Verde National Park

Conservation Concerns

In August of 1996, a great fire swept through Mesa Verde National Park. It was caused by a lightning strike in the Soda Canyon section, and it smoldered unnoticed for a day. The fire burned quickly, the flames reaching heights of more than 100 feet. Firefighters from neighboring areas joined the battle to save the valuable Far View archeological sites. After one week, the fire was at last contained. Although some sites suffered damage, most did not, because of the tireless efforts of the firefighters.

Although fire-damaged vegetation can eventually recover, precious archeological finds cannot be replaced. Money from new entrance fees has been allocated for the repair and replacement of exhibits and historic trails that were damaged in the fire.

The officials at Mesa Verde are concerned about other issues, too. As new archeological sites are uncovered, more staffing is needed to rehabilitate and maintain them. It is a policy of the park to preserve the original materials used in the dwellings of long ago. Sites are checked regularly for any signs of damage, and repairs are made before the problem becomes too big.

Protection of wildlife and vegetation is also a priority at Mesa Verde. Visitors are asked to report sightings of endangered or threatened species and to leave plants, rocks, and other natural or man-made features undisturbed.

Activities

1. Create a bulletin board about conservation activities in the park.

2. Pretend that you are a television reporter. Interview a ranger, geologist, and archeologist (classmates) about the 1996 fire.

3. Find out more about safety hazards in the park. Why is lightning particularly dangerous on a mesa?

Mesa Verde National Park

Special Features

The major archeological sites are among the park's special features.

Cliff House: This ancient sandstone dwelling contains 217 rooms with 23 kivas (ceremonial rooms). At one time, it was home to 200–250 people. It is believed that Cliff House was constructed by the Anasazi around A.D. 1200. Doorways in the structure were kept small to keep out cold air in the winter. The circular rooms or kivas were used as work rooms and social rooms, as well as for religious ceremonies. In the center of the kiva roof was a rectangular opening. With the aid of a ladder, the Anasazi climbed in and out of the room through the roof opening. Most of the living rooms were six feet by eight feet and about five and a half feet high. Wall paintings were discovered in Cliff House.

Long House: The second largest cliff home in Mesa Verde is located on Wetherill Mesa. It contains 150 rooms and 21 kivas. At one time it was home to 150–175 residents. The first part of the sandstone building was constructed at the rear of the cave. As the population grew, rooms were added at the front. Long House has a rectangular-shaped central courtyard that was called a *dance plaza*. This area was probably used for community meetings and ceremonies.

27

Mesa Verde National Park

Special Features (continued)

Spruce Tree House: This cliff house had 114 rooms and 8 kivas, and was the third-largest dwelling of the ancient Anasazi. The house was built into a natural cave and was covered by a large Douglas spruce when it was first discovered. The rooms had rectangular or T-shaped doorways. There were several storage rooms where the Anasazi kept their food supplies.

Mesa Verde National Park contains many other unique archeological ruins. Square Tower is one of the most photographed structures in the park. Pueblo Village, Balcony House, Step House, Mug House, and Badger House all provide visitors with insight into the lives of the Anasazi, the mysterious ancient cliff dwellers of Mesa Verde.

Activities

1. Imagine you are an archeologist writing for *Dig Magazine* in the late 1800s. Describe your discovery of one of the cliff houses of Mesa Verde.

2. How do you think Step House got its name? Write a story to explain your idea.

3. Pretend that you were a resident of one of the cliff houses. Describe a day in your life.

4. Do research and create a booklet entitled "Cliff Houses of Mesa Verde" based on what you learn.

Yellowstone National Park

History

Native American tribes once inhabited the land where Yellowstone Park exists today. They were the Sioux, Crow, Cheyenne, and Shoshone-Bannock. John Colter, a trapper and member of the Lewis and Clark expedition, is thought to be the first white man to explore and tell about the Yellowstone area in 1807.

Later, Jim Bridger, a trapper who was known to tell exaggerated tales, explored the area, too. When he told of boiling springs and other wondrous sights, many people did not believe him. In 1859, Bridger led a government expedition into the area to see the features he had described. Later, in 1870, a group of citizens from Montana also came to verify Bridger's claims. The members of this group were delighted with what they saw and agreed that the land should be under government control so that all citizens could enjoy it.

A United States Geological Survey team arrived in 1871 to take photos of the scenic wonders. Their photos, maps, and drawings were later shown to Congress in support of an effort led by Representative William Clagett of Montana to make Yellowstone a national park. On March 1, 1872, President Ulysses S. Grant signed the Park Bill and Yellowstone became our first national park.

Activities

1. Imagine that you were one of the first visitors to Yellowstone Park. You might have arrived there by stagecoach, horse and buggy, or horseback. Tell about your experience.

2. Pretend that you are Jim Bridger. Write a diary entry describing the sights you see at Yellowstone.

3. What if the Yellowstone land had not remained public property? What might it be like today?

Yellowstone National Park

Location

Yellowstone National Park covers a large area of northwestern Wyoming (2.2 million acres), and smaller parts of southwestern Montana and southeastern Idaho. Nearby cities include Jackson and Cody in Wyoming, Livingston and West Yellowstone in Montana, and Ashton and Driggs in Idaho.

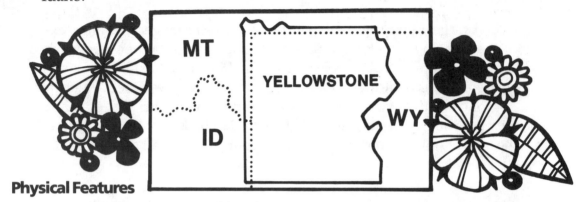

Physical Features

Yellowstone is filled with spectacular sights. The most unusual are the thermal features such as active geysers, geyser basins, hot springs, *fumaroles*, and *mudpots*. Fumaroles are holes in or near volcanic land areas that contain sulfuric acid. You can see hot smoke and gases rising from the fumaroles in Yellowstone. Mudpots are springs or pits filled with hot (usually boiling) mud.

Green forests blanket the mountain slopes and canyons. The beautiful Grand Canyon of Yellowstone has walls made of yellow rock called *rhyolite*. Dramatic waterfalls such as Tower Falls and Yellowstone Upper and Lower Falls are exceptional scenic attractions at the park. Petrified forests can be viewed along the northern section of the park in Specimen Ridge. Yellowstone is also known for its towering mountain peaks that seem to touch the sky, and its rocky cliffs, such as Obsidian Cliff, that look as if they are made of black glass. Clear mountain lakes, streams, and rivers traverse the park. A variety of scenic wonders awaits visitors to Yellowstone National Park.

Activities

1. Pretend that you work at one of the park's visitor centers. Give a short informative talk about the park's main physical features.

2. Make a mural of some of the major scenic attractions of Yellowstone.

3. Investigate and report to classmates about one of the following: the petrified forests of Yellowstone, the waterfalls of Yellowstone, or the Grand Canyon of Yellowstone.

Yellowstone National Park

Wildlife

Large and small animals abound in Yellowstone. Elk are the most common of the larger animals, and they are often seen grazing in various parts of the park. Some herds of elk and buffalo survive the bleak winters by grazing near the hot geyser basins. Bighorn sheep spend the winter high up on the mountain cliffs where the snow is not so deep. Moose find survival in the winter somewhat easier. They consume leaves, twigs, and bark from spruce and fir trees. Yellowstone Park is home to both the black bear and the grizzly. Black bears usually stay in the forest areas, while the grizzlies are often seen in meadows and alpine basins. The grizzly is much larger in size than the black bear.

Pronghorn antelope roam the park and survive mostly on sagebrush in the winter. Mule deer graze in the grasslands, while whitetail deer seek densely covered areas as their habitat. Smaller animals such as the snowshoe hare, beaver, wolf, marmot, ferret, and badger are year-round dwellers in Yellowstone.

Many species of birds are part of the Yellowstone environment. The lake and river areas are home to the common loon, white pelican, Canada goose, and trumpeter swan. The rare whooping crane is usually seen in the area of Gray's Lake, and the bald eagle, also on the decline, has recently increased its population due to environmental restrictions. The great horned owl is usually spotted flying to nest on cliffs or in trees. Many other species of wildlife enjoy year-round protection in Yellowstone Park, one of the outstanding wildlife sanctuaries in our nation.

Activities

1. As a class project, create a slide show called "Wildlife of Yellowstone Park."

2. Yellowstone has many excellent fishing areas. Research the streams, lakes, and rivers of the park. Explain why they are such a good environment for fish life.

3. Choose one of the animals mentioned above. Investigate this animal in more detail. Make a model of it in its habitat to display in your classroom.

4. Make a chart of the animal species living in Yellowstone that have been endangered or threatened at one time.

Yellowstone National Park

Plant Life

The mountains and valleys of Yellowstone are carpeted with beautiful forests and meadows. Plant life varies according to elevation. Trees cannot grow on the highest mountain peaks because of the poor soil, strong winds, and high temperatures. High alpine meadows, with small scrubby plants and wind-twisted bushes, are tucked among the peaks. During the short summer growing season, these meadows are sprinkled with bright wildflowers, such as shooting stars, mountain beauty, and forget-me-nots.

Growing up to the timberline are Yellowstone's thick evergreen forests. The lodgepole pine, the park's most common conifer, grows at the 7,600–9,000 foot level. Englemann spruce, Douglas fir, and ponderosa pine are also found at these elevations, together with purple lupine and red-orange Indian paintbrush, Wyoming's state flower.

On the lower slopes are groves of aspen trees. Columbine, Queen Anne's lace, and bluebells grow among them. Three varieties of cottonwood—narrowleaf, black, and plains—grow along rivers and lakes on the valley floors.

Yellowstone's plant life is an essential part of its ecosystem. The trees, shrubs, grasses, flowers, and mosses enrich and protect its soil, purify its air, and provide food and shelter for its wildlife.

Activities

1. Design a Yellowstone t-shirt which pictures some of the plants found in the park.

2. Research the 1988 fire that occurred at Yellowstone Park. What caused the fire? How was it brought under control? In what way did it affect the ecosystem at Yellowstone?

3. Make an illustrated chart of either five trees or five flowers found in the park. Compare habitats/elevations, sizes, growing seasons, etc.

Yellowstone National Park

Conservation Concerns

During Yellowstone Park's early years, tourists who had come to enjoy the park's natural beauty began to destroy it by writing their names on geyser cones, breaking rock formations to take small rocks home as souvenirs, and driving too fast along the park's roadways. Fortunately, most of these problems have been resolved, but as one of America's most popular national parks, Yellowstone still has tourist troubles. Most of the visitors to the park stay in what is called the "front country"—the area where the visitor centers, campgrounds, and geysers are located. Therefore, this area has become crowded. The park has many aging roads that need repair and some facilities that need upgrading. Although the park has raised its entrance fees, more funds are needed to cope with the challenge of constantly increasing attendance.

Another problem at Yellowstone involves wildlife conservation. Wolves and bears are the species most seriously affected. These animals need to be valued and respected by humans. Visitors are asked to not feed the bears so that the bears will not become dependent on humans for food.

Activities

1. Headline: CROWDS AND CARS BURDEN NATIONAL PARK. List some suggestions for easing the problems caused by too many visitors at one time.

2. Debate:
   VISITOR: The parks are here for people to enjoy.
   RANGER: Yellowstone is a park that is being enjoyed to death!
   Who is right? Defend your position.

3. Write a paragraph explaining why it is wrong to feed the bears while visiting Yellowstone Park.

Create a National Park
© The Learning Works, Inc.

Yellowstone National Park

Special Features

Geysers—Old Faithful: In many parts of Yellowstone, there is water beneath the surface of the earth. Some of this water comes up to the surface in the form of springs. But when the pressure mounts inside the earth due to hot *magma* (molten material beneath or within the earth's crust), the water becomes heated, explodes, and shoots up through cracks and holes in the earth. These hot springs are called *geysers*. Old Faithful, the most popular geyser in Yellowstone National Park, shoots out water in the form of a column. This column or *spout* rises 106 to 184 feet high into the air. Unlike most geysers, which do not have regular, predictable eruptions, Old Faithful shoots scalding water skyward every hour or so.

Activities

1. Research the meaning of the word *geothermal*. Name the four types of geothermal features found at Yellowstone.

2. Scientists and engineers are using geothermal energy to help us with our energy needs. Find out more about the steam power generators that produce electricity.

3. Write a story or poem about Old Faithful. Why do you think it is one of the most popular national park attractions?

Yosemite National Park

History

The valley, cliffs, canyons, and waterfalls of Yosemite were formed by glaciers millions of years ago. Continental shift formed its mountains.

In the 1860s, John Muir first saw the area. He wrote reports and letters to the U.S. Congress in support of its protection. In 1864, Congress gave the valley to the state of California to use as a park and recreation area. Yosemite was given national park status in 1890. At that time, the park did not include Mariposa Grove or Yosemite Valley. These were later donated by California and added to the park in 1906.

The area of the park known as Wawona was once an Indian campsite. Later, a hotel was built by Galen Clark for visitors traveling between Mariposa and Yosemite Valley. Clark became a protector of the area.

Activities

1. Write a thank-you letter to John Muir for his efforts to have the Yosemite area protected and preserved.

2. If you could visit, or could have visited Yosemite during any period of history, what time would you choose? Write a paragraph explaining your choice.

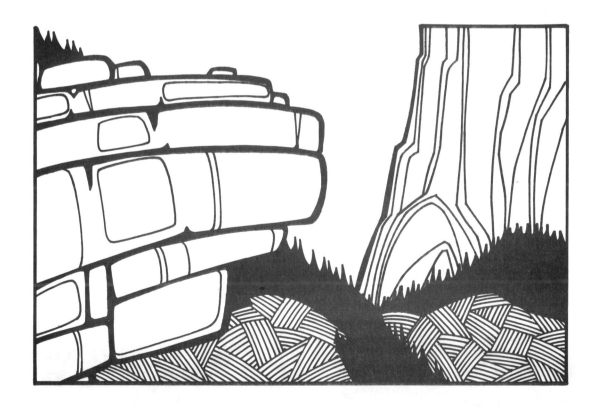

Yosemite National Park

Location

Yosemite National Park is located about 200 miles east of San Francisco, California, in the Sierra Nevada mountains. President Theodore Roosevelt called it "the most beautiful place in the world." Horace Greeley called it "The greatest marvel of the continent," and John Muir called it "nature's grandest creation."

Physical Features

Yosemite is probably the world's best-known example of a canyon carved by glacier action. The park stretches from 2,000 to 13,000 feet above sea level. There are glacially-carved lakes, cataracts, alpine meadows, spectacular mountain peaks, sheer cliff faces, and the second-highest waterfall in the world.

El Capitan and Half Dome are huge rock masses called *monoliths*. One stands at each end of the valley.

Activities

1. Do research to learn about Horace Greeley or John Muir. Summarize your findings and share them with your classmates.

2. Define *cataract* and *alpine meadow* as geographical terms. Draw an illustration of a cataract.

3. Find out more about El Capitan and Half Dome. Make a list of at least three facts for each and share your information with classmates.

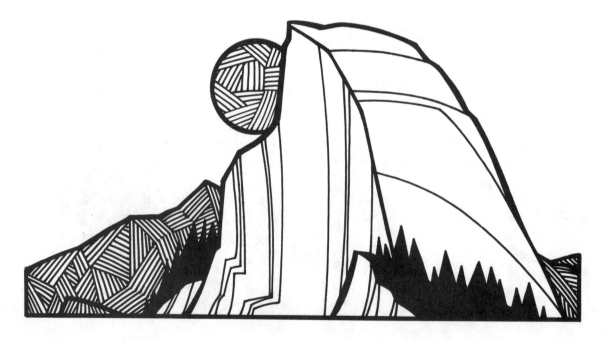

Yosemite National Park

Wildlife

Yosemite is home to hundreds of species of animals, many of which are commonly seen by park visitors. Brown, brook, rainbow, and golden trout swim in the lakes and streams. More than 200 kinds of birds live in the park's forests and meadows. These include the golden eagle, great horned owl, red-winged blackbird, California quail, and acorn woodpecker. Bold, noisy Steller's jays swoop down to steal food from picnic tables. Hummingbirds flash among the wildflowers.

Commonly-seen mammals include red and gray squirrels, chipmunks, raccoons, mule deer, coyotes, and black bears. Mountain lions, bobcats, gray foxes, and grizzly bears are rarer. Spotted and striped skunks are more often smelled than seen.

Visitors are strongly cautioned against feeding or disturbing the wildlife. Ignoring these regulations is harmful to the animals and often results in serious injuries to visitors.

Activities

1. Create a chart providing information on at least six species of Yosemite's wildlife. Categories might include the species' description, life span, diet, habitat, etc.

2. What signs indicate the presence of raccoons or squirrels? Describe or draw them.

3. Design a poster warning visitors about the dangers of feeding wildlife in Yosemite National Park.

Yosemite National Park

Plant Life

With almost 2,000 square miles of peaks, canyons, and broad valleys, ranging from 2,000 to 13,000 feet in elevation, Yosemite supports a great variety of plant life. Species range from tiny mosses and lichens to towering trees.

More than 200 different kinds of wildflowers have been identified in Yosemite including tiger lilies, monkey flowers, shooting stars, lupine, and California poppies.

The park's deciduous trees are found mainly in the Yosemite Valley. Willows, alders, and cottonwoods grow along the streams. Oak groves provide food and shelter for many animals. In the springtime, dogwood trees are covered with huge white blossoms. Yosemite's fall foliage includes the bright yellows and oranges of bigleaf maples and quaking aspens. Common conifers include ponderosa, sugar, and lodgepole pines; red, white, and Douglas firs; and juniper, cedar, and hemlock trees.

Perhaps the best-known of Yosemite's plants are its enormous, ancient redwoods, or giant sequoias. One of these, known as the Wawona Tree, was so large that a tunnel 8 feet wide, 10 feet high, and 26 feet long was cut through it. For 88 years, park visitors drove through this living tunnel; in 1969, however, the tree was felled in a winter storm. Redwoods have shallow root systems which are vulnerable to strong winds.

Activities

1. Debate the decision to cut a tunnel through the Wawona Tree.

2. Create a plant fact file on index cards. On each card, provide a drawing or photograph of one of Yosemite's plants and three facts about the plant.

3. Do any of the plants of Yosemite also grow in your area? If so, tell which ones. If there are none, can you guess why?

Yosemite National Park

Conservation Concerns

Yosemite is a place of great natural beauty and many recreational opportunities. It is also easily accessible from several large cities. For these reasons, the park is extremely popular, and it cannot accommodate the great numbers of people wishing to visit each year. Overcrowding has caused many problems, including damage to the park and its natural resources.

Care is now being taken to reduce human impact on the park. Limits have been set on the number of visitors, access to certain areas, and the use of private vehicles within the park. Trams and shuttle buses transport visitors to popular locations, and narrated guided tours are available.

In any popular natural area, there must be a balance between maintaining the site in its natural state and adapting it for use by visitors. Here are examples of problems that must be dealt with:

- Tourists being frightened or harmed by native wildlife such as bears and rattlesnakes.

- Trail use which causes erosion and disrupts or damages plant and animal habitats.

- The setting of controlled fires, which are needed to clear underbrush and deadwood, to control the spread of some plants, and to allow the germination of others.

Activities

1. Design a poster urging visitors to use trams and tour buses rather than private vehicles to travel within Yosemite National Park.

2. Make a poster that could be displayed in the Visitor Center encouraging visitors to respect park property.

Create a National Park
© The Learning Works, Inc.

Yosemite National Park

Special Features

Monoliths: El Capitan is the world's largest piece of solid granite. This "rock" rises over 3,000 feet above the Merced River, which runs through Yosemite. It is at the western end of the Yosemite Valley. Half Dome, the twin to El Capitan, is located at the opposite end of the valley. There are many other granite domes in Yosemite. In fact, the world's greatest concentration of monolithic domes is found in Yosemite National Park.

Yosemite Falls: At 2,425 feet, this waterfall is the highest waterfall in North America and the second-highest in the world. Yosemite Falls is 13 times higher than Niagara Falls!

Cascades and Cataracts: *Cataracts* are a series of steep rapids in a river. *Cascades* are small waterfalls usually occurring in sets. The Merced River has many cascades, waterfalls, and cataracts. This is especially true when the winter snows begin to melt. Yosemite is home to approximately one-half of America's largest waterfalls.

Mariposa Grove: The Mariposa Grove is a stand of giant sequoias. The largest of these is the Grizzly Giant. In 1958, this massive tree was 200 feet tall and measured 94 feet around the trunk. At an estimated age of 2,700 years, the Grizzly Giant is thought to be the oldest of its species.

Activities

1. Create an illustration of El Capitan or Half Dome.

2. Write a short story about an event taking place under or near the Grizzly Giant.

3. Is there an especially historic or famous tree in your state? Tell about it. How would its size compare to the Grizzly Giant?

Independence National Historical Park

Location

This famous park is located in Philadelphia, Pennsylvania. The official address is 313 Walnut Street. The park is part of the "Olde City" section of Philadelphia.

History

William Penn founded Pennsylvania in 1682 and created a government that allowed citizens to worship the religion of their choice and participate in making laws. People of varying ethnic groups resided safely in "Penn's Woods." The Pennsylvania State House (now Independence Hall) had a bell that was rung to announce public messages. This was the bell that was used on July 8, 1776, to proclaim the first public reading of the Declaration of Independence. It is now known as the Liberty Bell.

On June 28, 1948, an Act of Congress authorized the creation of a national park in this historic area. Led by Judge Edwin O. Lewis, an organization called Independence Hall Associates was credited with influencing the final legislative decision. In order to create the national historical park, historians knew that they would have to showcase sites of national importance and set criteria. Their initial themes for the park were the American Revolution, Philadelphia, the Capital City, and Benjamin Franklin. The historians also had to set park boundaries and identify buildings to be purchased. When they were purchased in the 1950s, the Dolly Todd House was a luncheonette and the Bishop White House was an insurance company office. On July 4, 1956, the administration of the park buildings began. At that time the sites that were open to the public were Independence Hall, Congress Hall, Old City Hall, Second Bank, and Carpenters' Hall. In later years, more sites were restored or reconstructed and added to the park. An excellent Visitor Center was built in 1975. It is a good place to start a visit to Independence National Historical Park, the birthplace of the nation.

Activities

1. Research facts about William Penn and the founding of Pennsylvania. Who were the Quakers? Present your findings to your classmates in the form of a skit. If possible, wear costumes for your presentation.

2. Pretend that you were on the committee to develop the park. Write a letter to your representative in congress offering reasons for the park's creation.

Independence National Historical Park

Historical Sites

Independence Hall: Independence Hall was originally built as the state house of Pennsylvania. At the time, Philadelphia was the capital of the colony of Pennsylvania. It took 24 years to build this red brick building. The Second Continental Congress met in Independence Hall to discuss the growing resistance to British rule. The Declaration of Independence was first read aloud in public in front of this building on July 4, 1776. This area is now known as Independence Square. Independence Hall is also where the writing of the United States Constitution took place in 1787.

Carpenters' Hall: The First Continental Congress met in Carpenters' Hall in September, 1774. Delegates from the various colonies came together to discuss the dislike of British rule and the resultant growing unrest. This building belonged to a carpenters' union called The Carpenters' Company, which still owns it today.

Declaration House: Thomas Jefferson lived in rooms in Declaration House that he rented from its owner, Jacob Graff. It was here that Jefferson wrote the Declaration of Independence. The house was not maintained, and this historical building was torn down. After its demolition, people realized what a treasure they had lost. The home was carefully rebuilt at the original location. Today, visitors can see rooms of Declaration House furnished as they were in 1776 in the days of Thomas Jefferson.

First Bank of the United States: This was America's first bank. Initially, offices of the nation's newly-formed government were housed in structures previously built for other purposes. Later, architects designed buildings such as this one specifically for government use. From 1797 until 1811, this was the nation's only bank. The inside of the building has not been restored and it is not open to the public.

Independence National Historical Park

Historical Sites (continued)

Second Bank of the United States: This building houses a portrait gallery featuring people who were prominent in America's early history. These include signers of the Declaration of Independence and of the United States Constitution, military leaders, and patriots such as Stephen Girard, who helped finance the new nation.

Old City Hall of Philadelphia: Located to one side of Independence Hall, this building, once a center of city business, served as the home of the Supreme Court of the United States from 1790 to 1800.

Congress Hall: On the opposite side of Independence Hall, this building matches the Old City Hall building. Once used as a courthouse, this building served as the home of the U.S. Congress from 1790 to 1800.

Todd House: This building was the home of Dolly Todd, the wife of a Philadelphia lawyer. Dolly's husband and son died during a yellow fever epidemic in 1793. Later she met and married James Madison, who was serving as a representative of the State of Virginia in the new nation's capital. Dolly Madison's home is open for tour groups only.

Christ Church and Cemetery: George Washington and Benjamin Franklin were members of this church, which was built between 1727 and 1754. Their pews still display their "name plates." As was the custom of the day, parishioners were buried within the church and in the small yard surrounding it. A few blocks away is the cemetery where Benjamin Franklin is buried.

Create a National Park
© The Learning Works, Inc.

Independence National Historical Park
Famous Residents of Philadelphia

Benjamin Franklin (1706–1790)

Benjamin Franklin came to live in Philadelphia as a 12-year-old printer's apprentice. He spent most of his life in this city, and is called "The First Citizen of Philadelphia." Franklin never sought public office, but was very interested and active in political affairs. He was chosen as Philadelphia's representative to the Second Continental Congress. In 1775 he became Postmaster General. Franklin was the only "founding father" to sign all four of the key documents concerned with the founding of America: the Declaration of Independence, the Constitution, the Treaty of Alliance with France, and the Treaty of Peace with England.

Thomas Jefferson (1743–1826)

Thomas Jefferson also took an active part in the proceedings of the Second Continental Congress. During a hot Philadelphia summer, he wrote the Declaration of Independence. It was approved almost exactly as he had written it. Jefferson retired from Congress in 1776 and returned to Virginia to work for land reform. During the Revolutionary War, he barely escaped capture by the British when they invaded Virginia. Thomas Jefferson served as the third president of the United States from 1801–1809. He died on July 4, 1826.

Independence National Historical Park

Famous Residents of Philadelphia

Betsy Ross (1752–1836)

A native of Philadelphia, Betsy Ross was the wife of Jacob Ross, a flag-maker and upholsterer. After Jacob died, Betsy took over his business. A committee from the Second Continental Congress came to Betsy and asked her to make a flag for the new nation. The committee members, which included General George Washington, presented their ideas in a rough sketch. Betsy suggested some changes and developed the final version with five-pointed stars. The "stars and stripes" design was adopted by Congress June 4, 1777.

George Washington (1732–1799)

George Washington is known as "The Father of His Country." He served as Virginia's representative to the Continental Congress in Philadelphia. He was appointed as commander in chief of the Continental Army. As General, he inspired his troops against great odds. The harsh winter that was spent in camp at Valley Forge is well known. Another famous episode is captured in a famous painting, "Washington Crossing the Delaware." Washington led his men in small boats to surprise enemy troops in New Jersey and win the Battle of Trenton. When he returned to Philadelphia in 1787 to serve in the convention that would write the U.S. Constitution, every bell in the city rang in greeting. On April 30, 1789, Washington was inaugurated as the first president of the United States. He served as president until 1797.

Activities

1. In addition to his role as statesman, Benjamin Franklin was also a successful inventor. Do research to learn more about his discoveries and inventions. Report your findings to the class.

2. Learn the meaning of the word *irony*. Do you think it is ironic that Jefferson died on the fourth of July? Tell why or why not.

Independence National Historical Park

Conservation Concerns

There are many treasured buildings, houses, and objects of historical and cultural value located in Independence National Historical Park. They all represent an important part of our nation's heritage, for it was here that the colonists began the dream that became the United States of America.

It is imperative that these historic sites be preserved for future citizens to visit and enjoy. There are, however, a number of problems that curators and historians must solve. Structures built 200 years ago were not constructed with contemporary life in mind. These buildings did not have central heating or air conditioning. They did not have modern plumbing, fire prevention equipment, or security mechanisms. In order to make these sites more accessible to current visitors, concessions often have to be made. Parts of buildings are sometimes changed in order to meet contemporary needs. These changes often are in conflict with history.

Curators must also face the threat of deterioration of public sites from atmospheric pollution such as vehicle emissions and acid rain. More than four million people visit these buildings each year, and repairs must continually be made. Taking care of these precious structures is a continuous project, but one that must be done in order to ensure their future survival.

Activities

1. "Should we change the appearance and/or structure of historic buildings in order to make them more accessible to visitors?" Debate each side of this controversial issue.

2. Find out about the Multi-Year Utility Improvement Project at Independence National Historical Park. What changes are involved?

Independence National Historical Park

Special Features and Exhibits

The Bicentennial Bell: This bell was a gift from the British to commemorate America's 200th anniversary (bicentennial). The Bicentennial Bell is located in the Visitor Center's bell tower.

Second Bank of the United States: Along with the extensive portrait gallery, visitors can enjoy tours led by park rangers. Another program available is "Brush with History," a children's program devoted to art history and United States history.

Visitor Center: In addition to the usual information desk, this building houses a theater which shows informative films. The Visitor Center is also home to a popular, interactive, computerized exhibit, "The Promise of Permanency." Appropriate for both adults and children, its theme is the United States Constitution.

47

Independence National Historical Park

Special Features and Exhibits (continued)

Churches: There are five churches within the Philadelphia National Historic Park and all have active congregations. Four of them have agreements with the National Park Service to allow visitors.

Activities

1. Working with marking pens on card stock, draw one of the buildings in Independence National Historical Park or copy one of the portraits found in the Second Bank of the United States. Then cut your drawing apart to make a picture puzzle.

2. Write a thank-you note to the British people for their gift of the Bicentennial Bell.

3. Design a board game to teach about the Declaration of Independence or the United States Constitution. Include all the parts and information needed to play the game, such as a board, game pieces, question cards, directions, rules, information on scoring, etc.

CALICO CAVERN

Section II
Create Your Own
National Park

Mustang Mesa

PRAIRIE TRAILS

Naming Your Park and Choosing a Location

The first section of this book provides information about some of our most popular United States national parks. In this section, you will become part of a cooperative learning group and create an imaginary national park of your own. As a concluding activity, your group will present a skit and other information about your national park during a special presentation called "National Park Day."

For this activity, you and other members of your group will choose a name, location, and nickname or descriptive subtitle for your park.

Type of park (national park or national historical park):

_____

Name of your park: _____

_____

Why did you choose this name? _____

_____

_____

Location (town, city, state, rural area): _____

_____

Many parks have nicknames or descriptive subtitles. For example, Yosemite is called "Sierra Wonderland." Acadia is called "Where the Mountains Meet the Sea." Brainstorm with your group and create a nickname or subtitle for your park.

_____

_____

IDAHO FLORIDA UTAH NEBRASKA
TEXAS VERMONT IOWA NEVADA

Mapping Your National Park

This is a map of Independence National Historical Park in Philadelphia, Pennsylvania. The park is located in an urban area, so there are many streets that help visitors locate the historic sites. In a rural setting, physical features such as rivers or mountains may help to mark special areas of a park. On a separate piece of paper, draw a map of your national park. Your map can be displayed during National Park Day.

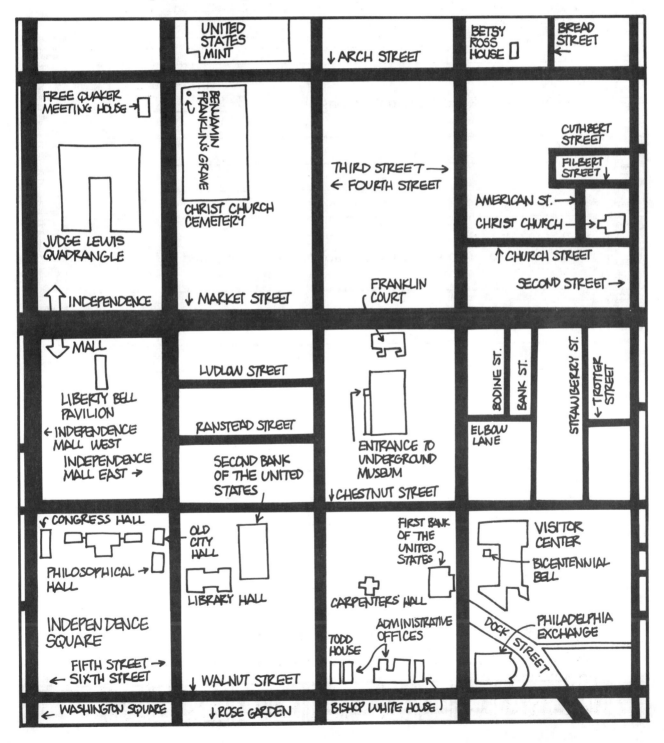

Create a National Park
© The Learning Works, Inc.

Group Worksheet: History

Brainstorm with your group several possibilities
for your park's history. Complete this worksheet as a group.

Who were the early inhabitants of the area? When did they live there?

_____

_____

_____

_____

Describe the park area as it looked long ago. _____

_____

_____

_____

_____

What historical events have taken place near or on this land? _____

_____

_____

_____

_____

Describe other groups of people who have lived in the area. _____

_____

_____

_____

_____

When did the area become a national park? _____

Why did the area become a national park? _____

_____

Group Worksheet: History
(continued)

Name any early explorers or other famous people who helped the area become recognized.

_____

_____

_____

_____

_____

How did your national park get its name? _____

_____

_____

_____

_____

Describe the history of any structures or artifacts found in your park.

_____

_____

_____

_____

_____

Throughout the years, how has the United States government helped to conserve the land?

_____

_____

_____

_____

_____

Group Worksheet: Wildlife

Read through the following questions, then, as a group,
complete this worksheet on your park's wildlife.

In the space below, list the wildlife species that reside in your park. Put
them into categories (for example, mammals, birds, reptiles, etc.)

Select two species and describe their homes in the park. _____

_____

_____

_____

What dangers do the animals in your park face? _____

_____

Select three species and describe the food that each eats. How do the animals obtain their food?

_____

_____

_____

Do research to discover what endangered or threatened animals might live
in your park. List them below and tell what could be done to help them.

_____

_____

_____

_____

Group Worksheet: Plant Life

Brainstorm with your group before answering the questions on this page.

In the space below, list the plants that grow in your park. Put them into categories (for example, shrubs, flowers, deciduous trees, cacti, ferns, etc.)

Choose two species and describe their setting within the park. On a separate piece of paper, illustrate their habitat.

_____

_____

_____

Are there any dangers to the plants located in your park? What are they? How is the plant life being protected? Could more be done?

_____

_____

_____

_____

Most plants are used by animals in some way. Choose three of your park's plants and describe how animals use them.

_____

_____

_____

_____

Group Worksheet:
What's the Weather?

Brainstorm with your group before answering the questions on this page.

In the space below, describe the weather conditions in your park. Describe each of the seasons. Remember that weather includes humidity, temperatures, precipitation amounts (rain, snow, fog), and wind.

_____

_____

_____

_____

_____

In the space below, make a chart showing the average high and low temperatures for each month in your park.

Describe how the weather or climate has influenced the plant life in your park.

_____

_____

_____

_____

Describe any unusual or specific weather occurrences in your park that make it "one of a kind."

_____

_____

_____

_____

Group Worksheet: Physical Features

Here are some physical features that you may wish to include in your park:

beach	fiord	mountain
bog	geyser	peninsula
canyon	glacier	river
cascade	glen	rock formation
cataract	island	swamp
cave	lake	valley
desert	marsh	volcano
dune	mineral deposit	waterfall

List five physical features of your park. _____

_____

_____

Describe the location within the park of each feature. _____

_____

_____

_____

Are any of these features used as recreational facilities? Are they habitats of endangered animals?

_____

_____

_____

_____

Create a National Park
© The Learning Works, Inc.

Group Worksheet:
Conservation Concerns

All national parks are concerned with the preservation and maintenance of their park sites. Brainstorm with your group the issues that must be considered in order to protect your park for the future. Use this worksheet to list three problems that exist at your park, the causes of these problems, and what can be done to remedy these problems.

Problem _____

_____

Cause _____

_____

Remedy _____

_____

Problem _____

_____

Cause _____

_____

Remedy _____

_____

Problem _____

_____

Cause _____

_____

Remedy _____

_____

Is there a clash between modern life-styles and human and natural history in your park? If so, explain what is being done to protect the past while updating the present (for example, modern facilities vs. building preservation, new construction vs. animal habitats, etc.).

_____

_____

_____

Group Worksheet:
Recreational Activities

Read through the following list and brainstorm with your group to determine which recreational activities you will offer at your park. Then create an information sheet that lets park visitors know which activities they will be able to enjoy during their visit.

- **Hiking:** List the types of hiking trails that are available in the park. Which are for beginners? intermediates? advanced hikers? Include any needed safety advice. On a separate piece of paper, sketch a trail map.

- **Scenic Driving Routes:** In your brochure, include a map showing the best way to see the important sights in your park. List the sights here.

  _____

  _____

  _____

- **Bicycling:** List the trails available for bicycling. What can be seen from the trails? What types of bicycles can be rented?

- **Horseback Riding:** Describe the areas in your park where horseback riding is permitted. Explain any restrictions.

- **Mountain Climbing:** When and where is mountain climbing permitted in your park? What special supplies are needed for this activity? Are guides available?

- **Fishing:** List the areas where fishing is permitted. Is a special license required?

- **Guided Walks:** Your brochure should include a map of the guided walks that are available in your park. What historic or important buildings or markers can be seen during the walk? If your guided walk is on a nature trail, tell about the natural habitats that can be viewed.

Group Worksheet:
Historical Markers and Monuments

Some areas of your park may be of historical importance. For example, perhaps an event took place there such as the birth of a famous person or the signing of an important document. Perhaps a famous person or group of people once visited your park, or there is a location within your park where a well-known work of art, music, or literature was created. With your group, create a marker or monument and describe what event, person, or group of people the monument commemorates.

Draw a design of your marker or monument in the space below.

What does the marker or monument commemorate? _____

_____

_____

_____

What materials will be used to construct the marker or monument?

_____

_____

_____

Facilities Information Form

Welcome to _____ National Park!

Our Visitor Centers are located _____

_____

Camping Information

Campsites are located _____

_____

Fee for use _____

Camping is open _____

Camping is restricted _____

Groceries, supplies, and gifts are available at _____

_____

Showers and restroom facilities are located at _____

_____

Lodges (Example: Jenny Lake Lodge)
List the names of motels, hotels, and lodges located in and near your park.

_____

_____

Dining (Example: Jefferson Restaurant)
List the restaurants and other dining facilities in the area.

_____

_____

Sight-seeing Excursions (Example: Kayak Adventures)

_____

_____

Equipment Rentals (Examples: canoes, skis, motorboats)

_____

_____

Rules for pets in the park are _____

_____

Warning Signs

National parks often post signs warning park visitors of possible dangers. Some warning signs seen at our national parks are shown below.

DO NOT FEED ANY ANIMALS IN THE PARK

SLIPPERY ROCKS

NO SWIMMING!

CAUTION: Stay on walkways around geysers, mudpots, and hot springs. Be safe!

WATCH OUT FOR FALLING ROCKS!

Alligators and Crocodiles Live in This Water

Now it is your turn to create warning signs for your national park. Consider the dangers that should be avoided and advise visitors on safety precautions. Use the space on this page to draft your ideas. Then make your final copies on construction paper for display on National Park Day.

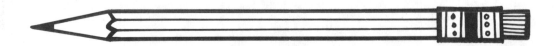

Travel Brochure

Travel brochures are designed to attract visitors to the places advertised. They use attractive photographs and drawings as well as eye-catching designs and lettering to get the reader's attention. Use the worksheet below to gather ideas. Then create a travel brochure advertising your national park.

What are the "highlights" of your park? How will you portray them in your brochure? What captions will you use?

_____

_____

_____

_____

List the reasons why people will want to visit your park.

_____

_____

_____

_____

How can visitors reach your park? List the major highways visitors can use to reach the park and describe any other forms of transportation that serve the area, such as bus, train, or ferry service.

_____

_____

List the services that are available in your park (for example, food service, medical assistance, lodging, rental equipment, etc.).

_____

_____

_____

What are the park's hours of operation? Do they vary according to the season? Give the address and phone numbers people should use to obtain more information.

_____

_____

Include a map which shows the location of your park.

Travel Poster

Create a travel poster to attract visitors to your national park. Think about the features of your park that you want to highlight in your poster. How will you display this information visually? You will also want to include some general information on your poster, such as your park's name, address, and phone number.

Use the space below to draw a small-scale version of your poster. When you are satisfied with the design of your poster, create a full-sized version on posterboard for display during National Park Day.

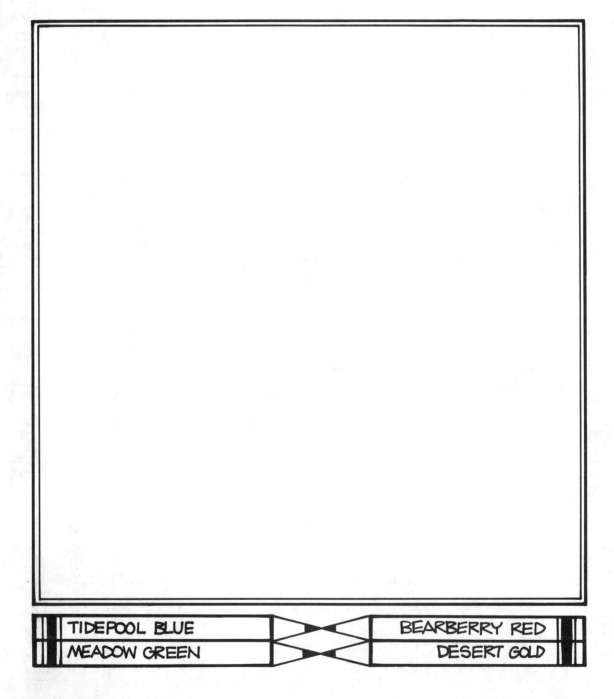

TIDEPOOL BLUE   BEARBERRY RED

MEADOW GREEN   DESERT GOLD

Special Exhibits

Many Visitor Centers in national parks have special exhibits such as:

- a collection of identified specimens and/or artifacts found in the park

- a "walk-through" exhibit featuring life-sized figures depicting a segment of life in the park's history. (Often these exhibits have automated sound systems that narrate what is being seen.)

- a video, film, or slide presentation

- an interactive display where the visitor is encouraged to ask/answer questions by pressing buttons, sliding doors, etc.

- live plant or animal specimens

- actors dressed in costume who reenact a particular piece of park history

Design a special exhibit for your park. Write a plan describing how you will create this exhibit.

Pick a Project

As a group, select a project from among the following ideas. Complete your project and include it as part of your display during National Park Day.

Design a Symbol or Logo

The image of a bald eagle is often used to represent America; Independence Hall makes people think of Philadelphia; and the cactus reminds us of the southwest. Design a symbol or logo that will represent your park to visitors. The symbol can be used in the form of a patch worn on the clothing of park staff members. It can also be included on park passes, souvenirs, and informational materials.

Diorama

Collect shoe boxes, gift boxes, or other small cardboard boxes to make a diorama. Create a typical scene from your national park. Draw or paint a backdrop, or cut one from a magazine or brochure. Add twigs, pebbles, or tiny toys for props. Label your scene to describe what is happening.

Design a Postcard

Create a design for a postcard that could be sold in the gift stores of your national park. Choose a feature that represents your park's uniqueness.

Compose a Poem

Write a poem about your national park. Use any style of poetry that you like, for example, rhyming, free verse, haiku, ballad, or couplet. Use figurative language such as similes, metaphors, and personification to make your poem more effective.

Simile: a comparison between two unlike things using "like" or "as."
Example: The frozen lake looked like a shiny mirror.

Metaphor: a comparison between two unlike things.
Example: In the winter, without mittens, my fingers are icicles.

Personification: a figure of speech in which a lifeless object is given human characteristics.
Example: The spring flowers danced on the hillside.

Design a Game

Now that you have created your national park, design a game that other students can play that will inform them about your park. It can be a board game, a computer game, or one played with pencil and paper. Make your game original and challenging! Bring your game to National Park Day and teach your park visitors how to play it. Use the worksheet on this page to record your ideas.

Name of your game: _____

Type of game: _____

Object of the game: _____

_____

How to win: _____

_____

Directions for play: _____

_____

_____

_____

_____

_____

Materials needed: _____

_____

_____

Create a National Park
© The Learning Works, Inc.

Encyclopedia Entry

The information in an encyclopedia is presented in a clear and direct style. There may be visual aids such as photos, paintings, maps, charts, and drawings to accompany each article. Sometimes a pronunciation guide is included. Cross-references or related articles may be noted at the end of each entry. These provide more information on the same topic that can be found under different listings. Example: Information about national parks can also be found under parks, national park systems, or the individual national park name.

On a separate piece of paper, create an encyclopedia entry for your national park. Make sure it provides important general information that will help other students learn about the major features of your park. Visual aids may be added to enhance your article. You may also want to create an oversized version for display on National Park Day.

Section III
Create a Skit

Using a Play Format

The script of a play or skit always contains two important elements: dialogue and stage directions. Dialogue is the words the actors speak. When writing dialogue, you should write the character's name and then follow it with a colon (:). Stage directions are the words that provide instructions to the actors on how to move on stage and how to recite their dialogue. Stage directions always appear in parentheses.

Example:

SAMANTHA: (In a nervous voice) I think I heard something move near the bushes. Could it be a bear?

ALEX: (Opens the flap of the tent) Don't worry. It's probably just the park ranger checking the area.

Practice writing dialogue and stage directions on the lines below.

_____ : _____

_____

_____

_____ : _____

_____

_____

_____ : _____

_____

_____

_____ : _____

_____

_____

Writing a Plot

A *plot* is the series of events which happens in a story. There are usually problems for the characters to overcome.

The parts of a plot are as follows:

Introduction: as the story begins, its setting is described and the characters are introduced.

Conflicts: As the plot develops, more information is given about the problem(s) faced by the character(s).

Climax: This is the point of highest interest or excitement in the story.

Resolution: In this part of the plot, problems are solved. Often, characters have been changed by the events of the story.

Create Your Plot

Work with your group members to create a plot idea for your national park skit. Some or most of the action should take place in your national park. What adventure or difficulty awaits your characters? How do they react to their problems and eventually solve them? Write your ideas on the lines below.

_____

_____

_____

_____

_____

_____

_____

_____

_____

_____

_____

_____

Developing Characters

Use this worksheet as you create and develop the characters for your skit.
Look at your plot to decide what characters are needed. Then think about
how each one might look, think, feel, and act. Use another sheet of paper if
you need more space.

Characters

Name and Age _____
Position/Role _____
Appearance _____
_____
Personality Traits _____
_____

Name and Age _____
Position/Role _____
Appearance _____
_____
Personality Traits _____
_____

Name and Age _____
Position/Role _____
Appearance _____
_____
Personality Traits _____
_____

Name and Age _____
Position/Role _____
Appearance _____
_____
Personality Traits _____
_____

Costume Ideas

Simple yet effective costumes can be made from things found around the house. Safety pins, staples, and tape can be used to fasten costume parts together. Full costumes are usually not necessary; a hat, scarf, or vest may be all that is needed to identify a character. Below are some ideas for costume creation.

Adapt Halloween or party costumes for use in your skit.

Vests may be made from paper grocery bags and decorated as needed.

Boots, belts, scarves, purses, and jewelry can add effective touches to your costumes.

Sheets, blankets, and towels make good skirts, aprons, hoods, and capes.

Sandwich boards may be made from cardboard, foam core board, or heavy butcher paper.

Hats of all kinds can be found at yard sales and toy stores. Painter's caps are often free.

Use a cap as a base for attaching paper ears, antlers, or antennae.

Plastic trash bags can be turned into costumes. Draw details on the bags with permanent markers. Use tape or staples to add paper or fabric trim.

Create a National Park
© The Learning Works, Inc.

Prop Ideas

Your need for props will depend on your story line, staging area, and amount of preparation time. First, list the scenes of your skit. Second, decide the basic props needed, and then those of secondary importance. Keep in mind that the props only need to represent an item or concept. The following ideas may be helpful when selecting and making props.

- Use solid-color plastic shower curtains, bed sheets, blankets, or large sheets of bulletin board paper for the background or for stage curtains. Details made of construction paper can be easily attached.

- Plant props can be made of paper, or silk and plastic plants may be used.

- Cardboard mailing tubes, paper towel rolls, and industrial paper supplies can be used for tree trunks, totem poles, fence posts, or logs.

- Corrugated boxes used to ship large appliances can be turned into building facades.

- Attach foreground scenery to chairs, wastebaskets, and music stands.

Now you are ready to create a short skit that takes place in your national park. Develop your characters and plot, then add costumes and scenery. Rehearse your skit before you perform it during National Park Day.

RAWHIDE RIVER

Section IV
National Park Day

RAINBOW REEF

DIPLODOCUS GULCH

National Park Day Planning Sheet

Use the forms and planning sheets in this section to help you
in your preparations for National Park Day.

Our national park name: _____

Date of National Park Day: _____

Time: _____ Place: _____

Names of group members:

_____   _____

_____   _____

_____   _____

Items needed for our park display: _____

_____

_____

_____

_____

_____

Props, scenery, and costumes needed for our park skit: _____

_____

_____

_____

_____

Sketch of Exhibit

Use the information on this planning sheet as you sketch the layout for your national park exhibit on a separate piece of paper. Your display should reflect your group's decision-making, creative thinking, and research skills. Look carefully at your assigned space to make sure that all of your items will fit. Make sure everything is clearly and attractively marked so that park visitors will have no trouble identifying your projects. Display maps and posters on the wall behind your table. Use your own original ideas to make your national park exhibit a special one!

Invitation Form

Design an invitation to tell your parents, relatives, friends, classmates, class-room aides, administrators, and other teachers about National Park Day. Here is a sample invitation to help you get started.

Dear _____ ,

    We have been studying national parks in the United States and would like to invite you to a special presentation entitled "National Park Day" to share what we have learned.

    National Park Day will be held on _____
                                                   (day/date)
in _____ . Our program will start at _____
        (location)   (time)
and continue until _____ .
                 (time)

    Working in learning groups, we have created our own national parks. Exhibits at National Park Day will include maps, models, dioramas, posters, and brochures. Skits will also be presented. We hope you will come and enjoy the things we have discovered and created.

Sincerely,

_____
                     and class

Park Lecture Planning Sheet

An important part of National Park Day is the exchange of information. When classmates and visitors appear at your exhibit, you must be able to describe the highlights of your national park. Refer to your worksheets from Part II for ideas and information. Then, along with other members of your group, plan an informative lecture on your national park. Decide which member of your group will talk about each feature of your park, such as your park's history, wildlife, physical features, and conservation concerns.

Use the space below to plan your national park lecture.

_____

_____

_____

_____

_____

_____

_____

_____

_____

_____

_____

_____

_____

_____

_____

_____

_____

Park Passports

On National Park Day, each group will be responsible for filling out passport pages with an "official stamp" and guide signature. Each park visitor will receive one of the passport pages showing that he or she has visited that park.

Example:

Park Name: _____

Location: _____

Official Stamp

The above stamp verifies that the passport holder has visited the park display.

_____
Signature of Park Guide

Design a passport page you can give to visitors of your national park. Stamps can be drawn or cut out of magazines. You can also use stickers that represent some special feature of your park.

Thank-You Letter

The following letter could be used to thank participants as well as those parents, teachers, administrators, custodians, media specialists, or others who may have contributed to the success of your National Park Day.

Dear _____ ,

    Thank you for helping our class with National Park Day. It was a huge success! We really appreciated your assistance. If you had a chance to visit, we hope that you enjoyed the exhibits.

               Sincerely,

            _____

               and class

Certificate of Participation

National Park Day

This certificate is issued to

_____

in recognition of his or her participation

in a unit on national parks.

_____   _____
date   *signature of teacher*

Evaluation Form

Now that your have had a chance to participate in learning about national parks in the United States and to create a park of your own, please answer the following questions and return this form to your teacher.

1. List three new facts or concepts that you learned from this unit.
   A. _____
   B. _____
   C. _____

2. Which was your favorite activity? _____

   _____

   Why? _____

3. Did you enjoy working with the others in your group? _____

   Were there problems? _____ If so, did they get resolved? _____

4. Did everyone in your group have an opportunity to participate?

   _____

5. What did you learn about yourself? _____

   _____

   _____

Section V
Park Potpourri

Our National Park System

Our National Park System is divided into 369 units. These units are located in the continental United States, Puerto Rico, Guam, Saipan, and the Virgin Islands. The National Park Service of the Department of the Interior is responsible for the management of these areas. These units are divided according to the following classifications:

Classification Title	Number
International Historic Site	1
National Battlefield	11
National Battlefield Park	3
National Battlefield Site	1
National Historic Site	72
National Historical Park	37
National Lakeshore	4
National Memorial	26
National Military Park	9
National Monument	73
National Park	54
National Parkway	4
National Preserve	15
National Recreation Area	18
National Reserve	2
National River	6
National Scenic Trail	3
National Seashore	10
National Wild and Scenic River and Riverway	9
Without Designation	11

Activity

Do research to find out which national park units are located in your state. Choose one and do research to write a one-page report to share with your classmates.

John Muir

John Muir (1838–1914) was a man who loved the wilderness. Born in Scotland, he moved to Wisconsin when he was a boy. Muir felt strongly that the wilderness areas in our country must be protected. In the late 1800s, the population of our nation stretched westward. Forests were cut down to make way for new towns, and the lumber was used to construct buildings. Dams were built across rivers, and railroads, bridges, and roads were rapidly constructed.

Muir was opposed to the new building because he felt that it was destroying the land. He asked President Theodore Roosevelt to set aside 148 million acres to be used as forest reserves. Later, Muir founded the Sierra Club to protect America's wilderness areas. Muir Woods in California was named in his honor.

Thanks to John Muir and others like him, today we are able to visit our beautiful national parks and enjoy the protected wilderness.

Activity

Here are the names of some other naturalists. Select two and read about them to discover their contributions.

Joy Adamson	William Beebe
Ray C. Andrews	Anna Botsford Comstock
John J. Audubon	Carolus Linnaeus
Liberty Hyde Bailey	Roger Tory Peterson
Daniel C. Beard	Ernest Thompson Seton

National Park Careers

There are many opportunities for individuals to work in national parks and serve as national park service rangers. Some of the careers that are available in the National Park Service are listed here.

Law Enforcement: These park rangers act as officers of the National Park Service. They enforce the rules and regulations of the park and protect the park. In addition, these rangers are asked to locate and rescue visitors who become lost in the park.

Maintenance Worker: Maintenance workers build, repair, and maintain park facilities. They also help to keep the park's roads and bridges working efficiently.

Fire Management Officer: These rangers work at preventing fires within the park. They also offer instruction to campers about fire safety.

Biologist: Biologists study the plants and animals of the park. They check on the habitats and environmental health of the park.

Administrator: The park administrator is responsible for budgeting money for the park, for hiring park rangers, and for planning for the park's future.

Anyone interested in learning more about national park careers should contact the Office of Personnel Management of the National Park Service. There is an Office of Personnel Management in each of the regional offices of the National Park Service.

Park Information Addresses

National Park Service
1100 Ohio Drive SW
Washington, D.C. 20242–0001

Acadia National Park
P.O. Box 177
Bar Harbor, ME 04609

Everglades National Park
40001 State Road 9336
Homestead, FL 33034–6733

Mesa Verde National Park
P.O. Box 8
Mesa Verde National Park, CO 81330

Yellowstone National Park
P.O. Box 168
Yellowstone National Park, WY 82190–0168

Yosemite National Park
P.O. Box 577
Yosemite National Park, CA 95389

Independence National Historical Park
313 Walnut Street
Philadelphia, PA 19106

Reference Materials

Books

America's Magnificent Parklands. The National Geographic Society, Washington, D.C., 1984.

Building the National Parks: The Historic Landscape Design of the National Park Service. McClelland, Linda Flint, Johns Hopkins University Press, 1997.

The Capacity for Wonder: Preserving National Parks. Lowry, William R., Brookings Inst., 1994.

The Complete Guide to America's National Parks. National Park Foundation, Washington, D.C.

Our National Park System: Caring for America's Greatest Natural and Historic Treasures. Rettie, Dwight F., University of Illinois Press, 1995.

Our National Parks. Reader's Digest Association, Pleasantville, NY, 1985.

Videotapes

Yosemite (45 minutes)
Holiday Video, Finley-Holiday Corporation, Whittier, CA.

The Scenic Beauty of America's National Parks (60 minutes)
American Visions, Cedar Rapids, IA.

Easy Access to the National Parks
National Parks Foundation, Washington, D.C..

Touring America's National Parks I and II (65 minutes)
Questar Home Video, Portland, OR

Internet Addresses:

http://www.nps.gov/
http://www.coolworks.com/showme/natprk.htm
http://www.llbean.com/parksearch/
http://bcaweb.bayarea.net/links/link23.htm
http://www.libertynet.org/~inhp/
http://www.acadia.net/w95026

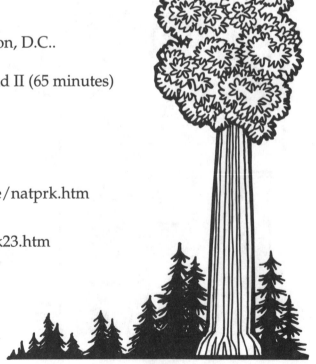